drinks well with others

other books by MikWright, Ltd.

hey, girl!

happy birthday . . . blah, blah, blah

who's your daddy?

your mother looks good . . .

MikWright . . . family style

mixed nuts

drinks well with others

MikWright

**Andrews McMeel
Publishing**

Kansas City

drinks well with others

04 05 06 07 08 TWP 10 9 8 7 6 5 4 3 2 1

ISBN: 0-7404-4747-9

www.mikwright.com

book composition by kelly & company, lee's summit, missouri

─── attention: schools and businesses ───

Andrews McMeel books are available at quantity
discounts with bulk purchase for educational, business,
or sales promotional use. For information, please write to:
Special Sales Department, Andrews McMeel Publishing,
4520 Main Street, Kansas City, Missouri 64111.

we would like to dedicate this book to
the folks behind the scenes at MikWright
that make our lives so simple:

to janis: thanks for keeping us informed
on all governmental activities that
take away our personal freedoms.
(for your information, we were the ones
who put cameras in our bedrooms.)

to jeanie: your extra efforts have
not gone unnoticed. it's your cooking
that has gone unnoticed.

to rudy: from a ditch in south dakota
to 2,400 square feet in plaza-midwood.
we love your every bite.
(p.s. rudy is a cat.)

acknowledgments

drinks well with others is yet another compilation of MikWright's not-so-serious and often cocktail-infused humor. all in good fun, *drinks well with others* conjures up images like grandma getting tipsy at the sight of communion wine, aunt violet lolly-gagging around the egg nog bowl at christmas, and mom's use of four-letter words after two glasses of wine.

we would like to acknowledge the family farmers of america for their participation in the production of grain alcohol. (and to that cute bartender down at the polar bar.)

cheers!

drinks well with others

having a good time.
wish you were here.

i miss you so much i could just puke.

excuse me . . . but we asked for
separate checks!
i don't know about everyone else,
but this will be the last supper
i eat here!

monica, dear, that was a
precious little story. now,
be a sweetheart and fix mommy
another martini.

little monica. sweet, precious, little cousin monica. evil! the devil in a low-cut, off-the-shoulder cocktail dress!

now, don't take our word for it. ask the broken-hearts club of men that she has created. not tall enough. not rich enough. monica is every daytime soap opera star wrapped up into a tidy little powder keg.

but we love her! who else would make out with a bush pilot at your wedding reception? who else would show you her latest reconstructive incision without a warning? who else would turn down three karats because they make a ring with four? (size does matter.)

monica is her own little reality show waiting for a primetime slot.

i don't usually drink while i fish.
i just drink.

finish up that dry turkey and
we'll go burn one.

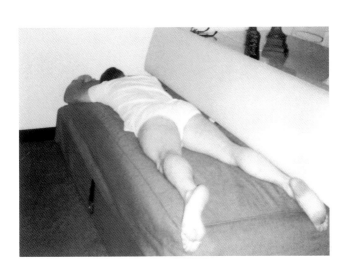

it wasn't until we got to the
islands that i got a glimpse
of his bad side.

mother of five.
grandmother of twelve.
drunk by seven.

grandma williams was a gem. with all those
kids and all those grandkids, she deserved a
cocktail now and again. (sometimes a little too
much now and then a little too much again.)

it's okay, though. we came out of it fine. dad's
a bartender, i'm a wine rep, and my sister has a
microbrew in the closet.

and . . . we all look forward
to church communion.

where the hell is my pickle fork?
i can't have anything nice with you
kids.

must you always be the
center of attention?

don't blame me, wanda!
i specifically told you it took
four "d" size batteries and not
to use it in the bathtub.

i'm sorry, it's not you . . . it's me.
well, it's not really me . . . it's you.
i mean . . . it's us.
well, it's not really us . . .
it's you.

you don't look a day over whatever
age you're claiming to be!

it's the same old song and dance . . .

everybody gets together for a friend's birthday and end up splitting the cost of the meal between them. here we go. somebody forgets the tax and tip and then the money goes around the table again until there's enough. oh wait, sally wants to use her credit card for the frequent-flier miles. david has a gift certificate and needs money back and deloris doesn't drink and is mad because they split the amount equally . . . and the birthday girl is now licking her ex-boyfriend's ear at a different table . . . and i accidentally regifted the bath salts sally gave me and now she's pissed. gawd!

she was nothing but a man-chasing
booze hound.
why can't you be more like her?

i can hardly wait to see him again . . .
this time with clothes on.

you got a problem?
kiss my ash!

for the record . . .
the only problem i have with alcohol is
that i'm running low on vodka.

we all have a sense of how much cocktailing
is actually good or bad for you. not that
we advocate public drunkenness, but it
can be funny to see fools born over one
too many a screwdriver. take our friend
who, while intoxicated, decided to hike
a hill to relieve herself. when she lost
her footing, all we saw was a pale white
ass tumbling down the hill.

enough, enough. this cocktail
ain't gonna refill itself!

every year during the holidays it's nice
to just relax and have a cocktail. and
then, after the holidays, it's nice
to just relax and have a cocktail.
cheers!

the holidays can be brutal.

running here, running there. this party,
that party. buying presents, returning
presents. ugh. somebody get me a cocktail!

(and, please not my uncle's homemade
dandelion wine—aka squirrel pee.)

every year we say "never again." the next
year rolls around and we do it again.
why? isn't it torture enough to make
the trek home so that we can talk about
the weather and argue about religion?

really . . . holidays should be spent with good
friends. there'll be plenty of opportunities to
see family at weddings and funerals.

make mine a double!

ma'am, the good news is your
furnace can be fixed by monday.
the bad news is your makeup
is all wrong.

how many times can the bitch
reuse that sign?

drinks well with others.

don't hate me because i'm fabulous.

```
now remember kids . . .
        no running,
        no diving,
and no salt on my margaritas.
```

there must be a thousand stories about parents, kids, and alcohol.

recently, while in seattle, a woman approached with a darling little story that goes like this . . .

when she was about four or five, she and her brother would spend time at their pool with their mother. because they weren't old enough to read, their mom tied different colored strings around the liquor bottles so that she could order them to "mix some of the red with some of the blue" to get a perfect poolside cocktail. genius!

i recall my first sip of alcohol. it was a little milky tasting since it came from my baby bottle.

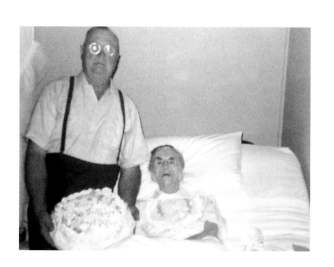

before we take the time to sing
happy birthday, could someone
check her pulse?

sorry about the birthday present.
my thirteen cats need shots, my
cousin is still in jail after
that jerry springer incident, the
trailer needs new underpinning,
and my whiskey collection is down
to airplane minis.

of course they laughed, you twit!
you told everyone that you were finally
back from hawaii and glad to be in continent.

dear abbey,
my son seems fascinated with my
daughter's easy-bake oven. do you
think i should have a cocktail?

liquor cabinet empty?
take a hint from eloise . . .
about one hour before your next
party, call everyone on your
guest list and tell them you're
running low on alcohol.

it's the oldest trick in the book . . . the book
on "how to fill you liquor cabinet."

you know, actually you're helping people
by not asking them to bring food. people
would much rather bring alcohol than a
covered dish. plus, they are probably just
going to give you the bottle back that you
gave them on the fourth of july anyway.

there's another handy trick we like to use. keep
the "good" empty bottles and fill them with
rail booze. watch your friends sip their
martini and brag about how much they like
their pretentious little vodka. (little do
they know they are drinking the dregs of
rotten potatoes soaked in bathwater.)

hey, i'm having a party. wanna come?
i'm low on tequila.

are you out of your mind sleeping
with someone you don't know?
save that for when you're married.

all right kids, mommy needs to run a few
errands, play eighteen holes of golf, and have
a cocktail with barbara. now, make sure the
house is in order for your father, and bobby,
don't forget to call the repairman about the gas
leak. i wrote the number on the matchbook by
the cigarettes.

it's a wonder we're alive.

once, when the folks ran an errand, we
lit the lawn on fire. (it was kind of hard
to cover up that scorched patch by the deck.)
and there was the time my baby brother walked
over to the neighbor's farm and climbed into
the pen with the bull. yikes.

inside, the antics were much the same.
if we weren't clowning around with dad's funny-
looking ribbed balloons, we were calling around
to see if anyone had prince albert in a can.
yep, we were freaks without a circus.

it's a wonder we made it through puberty,
but that's another story for another vodka.

i ain't got no list, santa.
but could you bring mama a complete
set of teeth, a veg-o-matic,
and a fifth of vodka?

give me a break officer! i'm en route
to the hospital with my illegitimate
daughter who has gone into labor
with god-only-knows whose kid.
plus, i'm missing *days of our lives*.

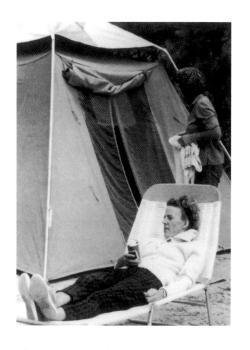

if a bear shits in the woods,
should i have a cocktail?

not a camper?

it's sort of strange, but some people love
roughing it. maybe it's the tepid showers or
watching the raccoons rifle through your
cooler. whatever it is . . . bring plenty of
beer. beer is a camping staple. twenty-eight
degrees outside . . . gimme another beer.
a hundred and four in the shade . . . beer.
no water to brush your teeth . . . beer.

camping is not for everyone . . . but the
hilton is and they have imports!

remember the office christmas party
when dottie got so plastered?
f.y.i.—the baby's three months
old and strongly favors floyd
from accounting.

those were the days.

not **exactly** fancy and free . . .
more like fancy and fifty dollars an hour.